The Latin Letters of
C. S. LEWIS

The Latin Letters of
C. S. LEWIS

*to Don Giovanni Calabria of Verona
and to Members of His Congregation,
1947 to 1961*

by

Martin Moynihan

Distributed by
Crossway Books • Westchester, Illinois
A Division of Good News Publishers

The Latin Letters of C. S. Lewis

Copyright © 1987 by Bookmakers Guild, Inc., 1430 Florida Ave., Suite 202, Longmont, Co. 80501, published in association with the Marion E. Wade Center, Wheaton College, 500 E. Seminary, Wheaton, IL 60187.

Originally published under the title "The Latin Letters, 1947-1961, of C. S. Lewis to Don Giovanni Calabria of Verona (1873-1954) and to Members of His Congregation," in *Seven: An Anglo-American Literary Journal*, Vol. 6, published by the Marion E. Wade Center and Bookmakers Guild, Inc., © 1985 Bookmakers Guild, Inc.

Quotations from C. S. Lewis's Latin correspondence copyright © C. S. Lewis Pte. Ltd. 1985.

Cover illustration by Robert P. Cording. Copyright © 1986.

Photo credits: Page 14, *Brothers and Friends*, by permission of the Marion E. Wade Center, Wheaton College; page 22, *And God Came In*, by permission of the Marion E. Wade Center, Wheaton College; page 38, Religious News Service; page 46, Burt Glinn/ Magnum Photos, Inc.

Distributed to the Religious Bookstore Trade by:

Crossway Books
A Division of Good New Publishers
Westchester, IL 60153

Distributed to the General Bookstore Trade by:

Bookmakers Guild, Inc.
1430 Florida Ave., Suite 202
Longmont, Co. 80501

First printing, 1987

Printed in the United States of America

Crossway Books ISBN 0-89107-443-0

Bookmakers Guild ISBN 0-917665-16-3

Library of Congress Catalog Card Number 87-070593

Contents

The Latin Letters of
C. S. LEWIS

A Refreshing Fragrance

WHEN I LEARNED from Dr Barbara Reynolds*— almost by chance, on our way to a meeting of the Charles Williams Society in London—that there existed in Wheaton a collection of letters in Latin from C. S. Lewis to a correspondent in Italy, I was thrilled.

That in our day and age Lewis should have brought off such a feat was one more feather in his cap. Like Dr Johnson's conversing with the French abbé in Latin. *Loquerisne linguam latinam?*, I was once asked by a Polish refugee in India, do you speak the

---

*Dr Barbara Reynolds is a co-founder and managing editor of *Seven: An Anglo-American Literary Review* published by Wheaton College, Wheaton, Illinois, and Bookmakers Guild, Inc., Longmont, Colorado. An annual review, *Seven* publishes articles and essays on the writings and influence of C. S. Lewis and six other well known British authors including Owen Barfield, George MacDonald, Dorothy L. Sayers, J. R. R. Tolkien, and Charles Williams.

Latin tongue? Alas, no. Yet doubtless there are many who *could* speak it and still more could *correspond* in Latin. But Lewis not only could correspond—he, it appeared, had actually done so, and done so in days when the art as a scholarly practice had died out.

But Wheaton is a long way away. And my second thrill was when by the kindness of Dr Reynolds and of the Administration of the Wade Collection I was able to see the letters in photostat.

How rapidly I drank them in! They were limpid, fluent and deeply refreshing. There was a fragrance about them, too, and not least in the way they were "topped and tailed"—that is, in their ever-slightly-varied formalities of address and of farewell. Each opening was an uncial, each closing a colophon, with its own distinctive flourishes.

My eye early lit on a passage in which Lewis has a characteristic tilt at the Renaissance and especially its destruction of everyday Latin in favour of a forced Classicism. In the battle between "Trojans" and "Greeks", Lewis was always with the Trojans, with the dunces so-called against the humanists so-called, with the true romantics against the false classicists. "If only", Lewis writes,

If only that plaguey "Renascence" which the Humanists brought about had not *destroyed* Latin—and destroyed it just when they were pluming themselves they were promoting it! We would then still be able to correspond with the whole of Europe.[1]

Yet correspond Lewis could and did. The letters lay in front of me: twenty-five in all. One or two a year, during the years 1947-61, the majority being from Magdalen, Oxford, and the last five from—or as from, *quasi*—Magdalene, Cambridge, both incidentally, as he points out, pronounced *Maudlin* (*Orthographia vero discrepant . . . sed idem sonant, i.e., Mōdlin*: they differ in spelling . . . but they sound the same).

There were no photostats of the replies; and the reason for this—it emerged from the last letter but one—gave me pause.

Evidently Lewis had been asked by the Casa Buoni Fanciulli (the Good Children's Home) of Verona if he could let them have the originals or else copies of the letters which he had received from his correspondent, their Founder, the Venerable Don

Giovanni Calabria. To this Lewis replies that he cannot. Much as he would like to help, it was his custom to consign letters to the fire two days after receipt; he had done so with Don Calabria's letters not because he did not value them but because he did not wish to relinquish to posterity things worthy of a sacred silence:

> For nowadays investigative researchers dig out all our affairs and sully them with the poison of "publicity"—to give a barbarous thing a barbarous name.[2]

This is the last thing, Lewis writes, which he would wish to happen to Father John who "in his humility and with a certain holy imprudence" had confided to Lewis things which Lewis would wish to remain undisclosed. Lewis asks that this be officially conveyed, *curialibus verbis*.

It is perhaps in line with this that, in one of his letters, Lewis writes to Father John ("what a layman ought scarcely to say to a priest"):

> You write much about your sins. Beware (permit me, my dearest Father, to say beware) lest humility should pass over into anxiety or sadness.[3]

Naturally, having read Lewis's *caveat* about those who dig up private matters, I immediately put myself in the dock. Was I thinking of doing just what Lewis deplored? But the Lewis letters are already open to view. And perhaps, as one who knew Lewis, I could help in introducing them to those who did not. Moreover, intimate though they were in tone, they did not, I found, contain any confidences which charity would wish to keep covered. On the contrary, they were to me, and might be to others, a source of renewed inspiration.

From the letters themselves (preserved in original in Italy by the archivist Fra Dall'Ora Elviro) it appeared that Father John was an Italian priest in Verona, the Founder of the Casa Buoni Fanciulli and the author of several publications, especially on the cause he was devoted to, Christian unity. He celebrated the Jubilee of his priesthood in 1951 (*quinquagesimum diem natalem sacerdotii tui . . . saluto,* writes Lewis, I salute the fiftieth birthday of your priesthood). At this point, Dr Reynolds came further to my aid with external evidence as follows.

First, there was, it appears, an article in *La Civiltà Cattolica* by Father Domenico Mondrone, S.J.: "Una Gemma del Clero Italiano, Don Giovanni Ca-

At "Little Lea," Belfast, Northern Ireland, 1919.

labria" (A Jewel of the Italian Clergy, Don Giovanni Calabria), which article, abridged and translated by I. G. Capaldi, was published in London under the title "God's Care-Taker" in the October 1956 issue of *The Month*. Later Father Mondrone wrote an article, again in *La Civiltà Cattolica*, "Don Giovanni e i fratelli separati"; and this subject received expanded treatment in a Lateran thesis by Eugenio Dal Corso, *Il Servo di Dio, Don Giovanni Calabria e i Fratelli Separati* (The Servant of God, Don Giovanni Calabria, and the Separated Brethren).[4]

All of these writings vividly bring out the devoted and truly saintly life of Father John as "a champion of the charity of the Gospel," and in particular how he founded, first, his San Zeno orphanage, the Casa Buoni Fanciulli, in 1907-08 and, later, his Congregation, The Poor Servants of Divine Providence, approved by his Bishop in 1932 and by the Pope in 1947.

The articles on Father John and the Separated Brethren tell of his theological and ecumenical activities and how he reached out to unknown correspondents in his concern for Christian unity and his desire to join with others in recalling men to Christ. We learn of several other correspondents besides

Lewis. But no correspondence seems to have been
so long-lasting, so affectionate, or so rewarding as
that between "lo zelato sacerdote cattolico e il de-
voto laico anglicano".[5]

What alerted Don Calabria was the translation in
1947 into Italian of *The Screwtape Letters*, published
by Arnoldo Mondadori. The work's title in Italian
was *Le lettere di Berlicche* and it was brought to his
notice by Father Genovesi, O.P. It so attracted Father John that he wrote to C. S. Lewis on 1 September 1947—and their long correspondence ensued!

Born in Verona in 1873 and growing up there as a
poor, fatherless boy, Father Giovanni had early con-
tacts with its Jewish community and also with Protestant acquaintances. His mother was very devout
and her support and her influence lasting. With the
years, Father John's ecumenical interests grew, end-
ing only with his death (he died after much suffering
and indeed a night of the soul) on 4 December 1954.

Evidently Lewis was apprised of his death by the
Congregation and was also sent a photograph,
which I have before me as I write. Acknowledging
this, Lewis wrote that Father Giovanni had left the
tribulations of this world and flown to our native
Country, adding:

Thank you for the photograph. His appearance is as I imagined: a conscious gravity harmoniously in accord with a certain youthful vivacity. I shall always make remembrance of him in my prayers and of your Congregation, too, and I hope you will do the same for me.[6]

Thereafter Lewis's letters continued, till within a few years of Lewis's own death, between Lewis and some inheritor of Don Calabria's place as a correspondent. The tone of Lewis's letters is uninterrupted; and they retain their interest to the last.

Five letters from Don Calabria to Lewis are extant (that is, I have seen copies of five and do not know of any others). The first of these, dated 1 September 1947, is the one which opened the correspondence. Lewis seems to have answered on 6 September and, hearing in return, to have written again on 20 September. The second letter extant from Verona is dated 25 January 1948; the third, 18 September 1949; the fourth, 17 December 1949; and the fifth, 3 September 1953. Their Latin is sometimes rough and ready but it always carries forward with great vigour and Lewis must have relished reading it as much as he relished the use of words himself. For example,

I think Lewis would have been delighted to meet in Father John's pages such words as *superlucrari* and *lucrifacio* ("to gain in addition" and "I make as profit") with their overtones of the Parable of the Talents. For his part, Lewis again and again gets the deliciously right word and he is not stymied by odd ones either: "typewriter" becomes *dactylographica machina*.

Father John continually expresses joy at Lewis's messages and at his work. He freely exchanges opinions with him and he is all the time encouraging him to write more. "Certainly", he writes on 18 September 1949,

> . . . you seem to me to be called to a special mission for the good of your neighbour . . . the gifts of heart and mind which you wield, the place which you hold among young students are sufficiently clear signs of God's will in respect of yourself. God expects from you that by word and deed you will bravely and sweetly bring brethren to the Gospel of Christ.[7]

In response, Lewis shared with his friend his hopes and fears, his experiences and his reflections and, when requested, his views on life, affairs and theology.

T W O

Unity and Charity

CHRISTIAN UNITY, although it by no means monopolises their correspondence, sets its keynote. *Ut omnes unum sint,* that they may all be one (*John* XVII 21): Lewis thanks Father John for his words and his publications on this theme. For his part, he assures Father John that no day passes when he does not himself pray that prayer—*and pray it from the heart.*

There is no schism, Lewis agrees, without sin. It does not follow, he thinks, that sin is schism's whole cause. Tetzel, on the one side, and Henry VIII, on the other, were indeed lost men. But what of Thomas More and Tyndale? I have recently, says Lewis (25 November 1947) read through the whole works (*sic*) of the one and the other. Both were the saintliest men whose shoes Lewis felt unworthy to unloose. But they differed; and their dissension arose not from faults of theirs or ignorance but rather from their very virtues and from their faith's truest depth. It was what was best in each that placed them most at variance. Lewis concludes that for him this is a mystery—perhaps more so, he adds, than it is for Father John. He alludes to the Psalmist: "Thy judgments are an abyss".

To write of the Pope, as Father John had, as "the point of meeting" (*il punto di incontro*) seemed to him to beg the question since it was around the Papacy, Lewis wrote, that almost all difference of opinion had revolved.[8] However, pending the union of faith and of order, all the more should the union of charity be ours. And, in this spirit of charity, joint resistance against common foes is, Lewis wholeheartedly agrees, the way ahead. For:

> Disputations do more to aggravate schisms than to heal them: common action, united prayer, united courage and even (if God so will) united deaths—these will make us one.[9]

Having shared their minds on this subject of Christian unity, the two correspondents, it seems, passed on to other things. But there are echoes of the subject throughout. Thus, writing of the Hitlers of our times, Lewis suggests that these may prove, by God's overruling, to have been hammers, hammers for good, used by God to weld us (us, who have refused less severe remedies) into unity. For, he writes (in a rhythm reminiscent of Abraham Lincoln):

. . . those who suffer the same things from the same people for the same cause can hardly fail to feel love among themselves.[10]

There is one other passage in which Lewis turns to the theme of unity—and to the terrible facts of disunity—and that is when he reports that he is holiday-bound and soon to cross over (if it shall please God) into Ireland:

. . . to my birthplace and most sweet refuge, so far as loveliness of landscape goes and mildness of climate—although most dreadful because of the strife, hatred and often civil war between dissenting beliefs. There indeed both your people and ours "know not by what Spirit they are led". They take lack of charity for zeal and mutual ignorance for orthodoxy.[11]

In his study at the Kilns, 1960.

Elsewhere he writes, let us keep the bond of charity "which, alas, your people in Spain and ours in Northern Ireland do not".

From one of Father John's Letters (3 September 1953) it is evident how vibrant a chord Lewis awoke when he wrote of zeal mistaken for charity and mutual ignorance mistaken for orthodoxy. "These words has the Spirit inspired you with! . . . Happy you (say I, and shall say) whom God wills to use in the execution of His works."[12]

These bonds of love, needless to add, extend far beyond the realm of public affairs; and nothing is sweeter in this correspondence than the evidently growing and heartfelt affection between the two never-to-meet writers. In a letter of 17 March 1953, Lewis writes that it

> . . . is a wonderful thing and a strengthening of faith that two souls differing from each other in place, nationality, language, obedience and age should have been led into sweet familiarity: so far does the order of spiritual beings transcend the material order.[13]

Throughout the letters there is a happy intermingling of serious reflection and day-to-day needs.

Lewis cannot reply at once, he writes, because he is engulfed in the return of undergraduates at the beginning of term and so is experiencing the curse of our First Parent—"in the sweat of thy face shalt thou eat bread".

Nor do the seasons pass unnoticed, nor the weather. In the Spring of 1948, all Nature, he writes, is visibly emblematic of the joy of Easter. Evil days notwithstanding,

> Nature herself—the very face of the earth now truly renewed after its own manner of renewal—bids us *Rejoice*![14]

At times Lewis has less cheerful notes to strike:

> I work under great difficulties. My house is unquiet, rent with women's quarrels. "I have to dwell in the tents of Kedar." My aged mother (*grandaeva mater*), worn out by long infirmity, is my daily care. [5]

However, if he tells Father John all this, it is not, he quickly adds, "by way of complaint but lest Father John should believe that he has the time to be writing books". Moreover at fifty Lewis feels that his talent is decreasing and his readers less pleased than they used to be. So,

> . . . if it shall please God that I write more books, blessed be He. If it shall please Him not, again, blessed be He.[16]

THREE

Great Truths of the Christian Faith

NOTHING IN THESE LETTERS is perhaps more constant than Lewis's own courageous constancy. The great truths of the Christian faith—its great topics, one might say—are ever adduced to fortify daily life. Language which at first might sound trite grows, under the weight of trouble (*aerumna*), glorious. *Nil desperandum*—we laugh at first, at that schoolboy phrase. But—never despair—we stay to pray, when it holds its own through suffering.

Lewis himself must have enjoyed the mere fact of writing in Latin. In his salutations he soon moves from the tentative to the pronounced, interacting here with Father John. St Peter tells us to be courteous (1 *Peter* III 8, A.V.). Be then truly so. And how soon the courtesies pass into most real affection! "Reverend Father," "Dear Father," "Father most beloved"—these and still more the farewells would repay a study in themselves. The Italian commentators remark on this note of filiality, here and elsewhere in the letters; and it elicits from them a cry of spontaneous joy.

Sometimes—indeed not seldom—Lewis has been taxed with pastiche. I would rather call it repossession. In a current context, an old mode, a remembered phrase can be re-appropriated and can be lived out, to fresh advantage. I experienced something of this in the War:

The *reeking tubes*—you saw them reek.[17]

In this respect too, Lewis reminds me of what is told of Chesterton. You would see G.K.C. smile; then make a quick sketch; then look at the sketch he'd made—then smile again, indeed shake with suppressed laughter. Lewis knew old usage; he reposseses it; and the thing, repossessed, becomes a force in his life and in the life of others.

It is just so, too, with our age-old liturgy and the Church's calendar. In these letters, Lewis is seen to be living the liturgy and living the calendar. He tells Father John he will be remembering him at Holy Communion—and prays Father John ever to make remembrance of *him*. He writes of our going to

Bethlehem at the Feast of the Nativity, and of Christ's ascension, on Ascension Day. He invokes intercession—up till the River of Death, and beyond. Lewis is sometimes referred to as an Ulster Protestant. Ulsterman, yes, like, say, Field-Marshal Lord Alexander and others. But if bigotry is implied, then hardly so. For although, writing to Father John, he writes of "yours" and "ours", because the Continent sees Christendom as either Catholic or Reformed, the Church which he was writing from was ever seeking, as the Ecclesia Anglicana, to be both Catholic and Reformed. In this respect Lewis's spirit is that of his admired author, Sir Thomas Browne, and his book the *Religio Medici*. Lewis himself, throughout these letters, draws inspiration from Christendom's primary sources, from Holy Writ and from the early Fathers, and he always does so as from a common heritage.

We have learned from Dr Derek Brewer how Lewis would recommend his pupils to read the Vulgate as a simple way of increasing knowledge of Latin and Scripture simultaneously. In this correspondence Lewis himself quotes texts from memory, *currente calamo*, in his own Latin. He once writes that his Vulgate is not to hand. The freedom he thus uses results from mastery of his source, not unfamiliarity. When he writes about the tents of Kedar he is latinizing Coverdale (The Book of Common Prayer); when about God's judgments as an abyss, he is alluding to the Vulgate and the Septuagint. In the result many a familiar meaning is in words of his own. Thus *caliga*, a leather shoe, is Lewis's, in place of the Vulgate's *corrigia*, a shoe-latchet or *calceamenta*, shoes.

There is one word which stands out as indubitably the Vulgate. The Authorised Version and the Douai give in 1 *Peter* I 8, joy "unspeakable": "in whom . . . though now ye see Him not, yet believing ye rejoice with joy *unspeakable*". "*Credentes autem*", runs the Vulgate, "*exultabitis laetitia inenarràbili*", with joy unnarratable, joy beyond telling. I cannot but think it more than a coincidence that this word, in its English form, "inenarrable", was to the fore in the Twenties. Sir Robert Bridges, the then Poet Laureate, canvassed with others whether the stress in English should fall on the third or the second syllable, giving his vote, I think, to the second, as in the line:

The inénarrable (ineénarrable) content of delight

that is, of delight beyond our telling, beyond narrat-
ing. Lewis, I fancy, recollected this and, as we shall-
see later, uses the word with all the resonance of its
context in the Vulgate.

F O U R

Grace and Forgiveness

IN ONE LETTER Lewis writes to Father John that of all the Deadly Sins the one which most beset him was—what I fancy few of his friends would imagine—Sloth: to quote Chaucer,

>the synne of Accidie.

If so, how powerfully the sin was overcome by Grace! Yet we should think, here, rather of the grace of cheerfulness than of energy. Spiritually, sloth is the torpor which spreads from dolour; and of dolour, dating from his mother's death when he was so young, how much Lewis knew! He, again like Chesterton, was inspired to cast it off—and to help others in doing so. (Readers of Lewis's correspondence with his lifelong friend, Arthur Greeves, will remember that in his early life Lewis found Pride, not Sloth, his besetting sin. See p. 339 of *They Stand Together*, ed. by Walter Hooper, Collins 1979.)

The helping of others is never far from Lewis's reflections. The books which he writes he hopes will fill some gap. Father John may not find the Narnia stories of interest—but see if they may not please his "buoni fanciulli". Or his book on Prayer: it is not for the advanced but to help the beginner. It was because he found few books on it for *beginners* that he "tackled the job" (*laborem aggressus sum*). How characteristic! Where the line was thinnest, there went Lewis.

He is charitable to the younger generation. They may seem headstrong but they show courage; also are they not more compassionate than heretofore, in their caring for the poor and the afflicted? We older men, he says to Father John, must be careful not to be *laudatores temporis acti*, praisers of the past. The old tag—but it comes in well.

He grounds his own goodwill, and that of all men, upon its foundation in Christ. More than once he steadies himself, and Father John, by recalling Christ's words that there will be wars and rumours of wars: "see that ye be not troubled". And from this he faithfully deduces not supineness but continuance in well-doing—well-doing not remotely but to our spatial neighbour:

Let us beware lest, while we torture ourselves in vain about the fate of Europe, we neglect either Verona or Oxford.

In the poor man who knows at my door, in the ailing mother, in the young man who seeks my advice, the Lord Himself is present. Therefore let us wash His feet.[18]

Lewis does not share Father John's feeling that the times are at their worst. But, if they were, what were that but our Salvation drawing nigh? However, they indeed are evil and in nothing so much as being worse than pagan times. For the pagan-before-Christ had a virtue which the apostate-from-Christ can never have. The early pagan and the late apostate are as virginity to adultery. Many apostates have fallen away not only from the law of Christ but from the law of Nature too. For, whereas Faith gained perfects Nature, Faith lost corrupts it. So, to Lewis it seems, in reply to Father John, that evangelism, faced with people who no longer feel a sense of sin, must begin by re-eliciting awareness of law. The great bane is moral relativity. We must overcome that, before we move against atheism.

Clearly one of Lewis's best-loved books was *The*

Imitation of Christ. And some of the spirit of that priceless volume has breathed itself into these letters, especially when they apply, as they so often do, the words of Scripture. But Lewis cannot find in *The Imitation* what he expected to trace thither—and does Father John know the source?—

Amor est ignis jugiter ardens, Love is an undying fire.

Many times the Latin words carry a force and a flavour which repay examination. *Immanitas:* that enormity, that lack of measure, that alienation from good, from the good spirits, the *Manes*—how redolent of *The Abolition of Man* and *That Hideous Strength*! Or *gustationes*: Lewis wishes Father John all the "relishes", all the "foretastes" which temporal blessings afford. The joys of this life—they are not more, but neither are they less, than "antepasts" of heaven. Lewis loads even his farewells with the nourishment of doctrine. Christ is very God and very Man—indeed the only True Man because all men after the Fall have been but half-men. (Shades of Ransom and the bent men!) This doctrinal conclusion elicits the warmest welcome and endorsement from Father John.

To Father John Lewis reports two great experiences. One was his own, one a friend's. His own he
suggests he may owe—who can tell?—to prayers by
Father John on his behalf. The experience, in 1951,
was a sudden and profound awareness of forgiveness of sins, of his own sins, of his own liberation:

> I long *believed that I believed* in the forgiveness
> of sins. But suddenly (on St Mark's Day) this
> truth appeared in my mind with such manifest
> light that I perceived that never before (and
> that after many confessions and absolutions)
> had I believed it with my whole heart.[19]

Lewis then goes on to request the liberty of coun-
selling Father John. Do not let humility and contri-
tion pass over into sadness. For Christ has abolished
the handwriting (*chirographia*) that was against us.
Twice Lewis excuses himself—was he not a layman
and a junior? But, out of the mouths of babes. Indeed once, in Balaam's case, out of the mouth of an
ass! (Elsewhere, Lewis had written of the Magdalene
as his Patron: and she—did he recollect in this context?—was prefigured in Old Testament typology as
a type of the Gentile Church by Balaam.) Finally, at
the end of his filial entreaty he again asks Father

In his Cambridge office, 1958.

John's pardon, this time for his *balbutiones*, his stammerings. *Balbutiones*, with its flavour, etymologically, of barbarisms—how this word suggests both the child in grace and the good barbarian and withal those admonishings in the New Man wherein is neither Greek nor Barbarian, bond nor free!

The second experience befell Lewis's friend—his aged Oxford confessor. It was an experience, and an example, of holy dying. I feel orphaned, Lewis writes, because my aged confessor and most loving father in Christ has just met death.

> While he was celebrating at the altar, suddenly after a most sharp but (thanks be to God) very brief attack of pain, he expired and his last words were "I come, Lord Jesus".[20]

Impossible not to recall the last chapter of Charles Williams's novel *War in Heaven*. *Introibo*—I will go in to the altar of God, to God who giveth joy to my youth: *ad Deum qui laetificat juventutem meam*. Like the Archdeacon in Charles Williams's fiction—"I suppose they will say he had a weak heart"—Lewis's aged confessor, when summoned to his Exodus, most gladly responded.

As you read and re-read these letters you get an ever-growing sense of the significance which should be attached to prayer. The word *insta* brings this home. Persevere with? Press on with? How would Lewis have rendered his own Latin? And suddenly you remember its echoes in the Epistles: "patient in tribulation; continuing *instant* in prayer", *In tribulatione patientes Orationi instantes* (*Romans* XII 12).

But stronger still, in earth and air—

has not Christopher Smart sung in his *Song to David?*—

> But stronger still, in earth and air,
> And in the sea, the man of prayer,
>   And far beneath the tide:
> And in the seat to faith assigned
> Where ask is have, where seek is find,
>   And knock is open wide.

But *is* knock "open wide"? Lewis puts to Father John the same difficulty which he later put to the Oxford Clerical Society in his paper on 8 December 1953, "Petitionary Prayer: a problem without an answer". I will not traverse it here[21] but it does not appear that Lewis received any answer which, to his mind, resolved the difficulty.

In her introduction to her translation of *Orlando Furioso*, Dr Barbara Reynolds has shown us how Ariosto interwove Classical, Celtic and Carolingian elements into his epic. This combination of old and new in a Christian synthesis was something Lewis always valued—it was why he compared Tolkien with Ariosto—and it was something, too, which in his own way he also exemplified. It is not therefore surprising that in these letters along with scriptural allusion we find, side by side, classical quotation. Sometimes this juxtaposition produces a novel effect. *Sursum corda*, lift up your hearts! We are not expecting this quotation from the liturgy to be followed, but followed it is and that immediately, by Virgil:

> forsan et haec olim meminisse juvabit.

How familiar yet how vivid! "Perhaps one day it will be a joy to recall even this." The great utterance takes on a fresh vigour from its new Christian context.

Horace is also laid under tribute, in a letter where Lewis tells that he is writing a book on the Four Loves:

Pray for me that God grant me to say things helpful to salvation or at least not harmful. For this book-to-be, *The Four Loves*, is "a work full of dangerous hazard", as Flaccus wrote.[22]

Flaccus—how nice, in a letter to Italy! Yeats, one recalls, said Horace. But he balanced that by singing, not of Cicero, but Tully:

> Horace, there by Homer stands,
>   Plato stands below,
> And there is Tully's open page.
>   How many years ago
> Were you and I unlettered lads
>   *Mad as the mist and snow?*

FIVE

No Farewells Are Final

A S THE LETTERS APPROACH the 1960's, so there is a sense of change, not because Lewis, from 1954 onwards, is writing to a new correspondent following Father John's death, but because of actual changes in Lewis's own world. And, first of all, the move from Oxford to Cambridge.

Earlier, Lewis had said that Italy had one advantage over Britain. In Italy, Communists declared themselves to be atheists and so people knew where everyone stood. In England, however, extremists all too often claim to be advancing the kingdom of God and present themselves in sheep's clothing.

When it comes to Oxford and Cambridge, Lewis (before he had moved to Cambridge) wrote:

> The Christian Faith counts for more, I think, among Cambridge men than among us; the

Communists are rarer and those pestilential philosophers whom we call Logical Positivists are not so powerful.[23]

And now we must change our notes to tragic. The word *aerumna*, trouble, re-appears (16 April 1960) and does so with stark brevity: "I am in much trouble". Lewis does not specify. But earlier he had said how, after a remission of two years, his wife Joy's lethal disease, *letalis morbus*, has returned. Even so, he adds, you would not believe how many joys have been experienced amid these troubles. "And what wonder? For has He not promised to comfort those who mourn?" So here. "I am in much trouble. Nonetheless let us lift up our hearts: for Christ is risen." It is impossible, reading these letters, not to be moved and moved equally by grief and admiration. Going through the vale of misery Lewis uses it for a well: and the pools thereof are filled with water. Fortitude, what Christian fortitude! And with his bicentenary freshly in mind, it is natural here to think once more of Dr Johnson.[24]

Lewis, as I have noted, never hesitates to use the traditional phrase or to utter the appropriate observation. This was characteristic and intentional. We are to follow the Way. But Lewis goes to the ultimate. In the Valley of the Shadow, he does not give up. He bears it out, "even to the edge of doom". And why? "Love's not Time's fool."

It seems to me that there is a special poignancy in his Latin at the close, a Latin the very rhythm of which is infinitely moving. But there is no want of poignancy in the English either. And surely our eyes and hearts and prayers will follow Lewis as he writes this last sentence of these letters of his, some eight months after Joy's death on 8 April in the Year of Our Salvation 1961:

> I know that you will be pouring out your prayers both for my most dearly-longed for wife and also for me who—now widowed and as it were halved—journey on, through this Vale of Tears, alone.[25]

How grateful I feel to Wheaton College and to the Archivist in Verona for having assembled and preserved this C. S. Lewis/Don Calabria correspondence! Looking back over it all you see that Lewis and Father John unite with each other in teaching a ministry of charity—and about each of them you

In his rooms at Cambridge, 1958

spontaneously add what Chaucer wrote of his Parson,

He taught but first he practised it hymselve.

correspondence was itself a part of this ministry of theirs. It must often have been exacting yet it was also sustaining. And its essence was mutual intercession. Lewis who was a great Arthurian would agree that it is the prince of Arthurian poets who has expressed this, the life of prayer, better than most (not inappropriately, in the *Morte*):

But thou,
If thou should'st never see my face again,
Pray for my soul. More things are wrought
    by prayer
Than this world dreams of. Wherefore, let
    thy voice
Rise like a fountain for me night and day.
For what are men better than sheep or goats
That nourish a blind life within the brain
If, knowing God, they lift not hands of
    prayer
Both for themselves and those who call them
    friend?

For so the whole round world is every way
Bound by gold chains about the feet of God.
But now farewell.

Farewell: but christianly speaking, no farewells,
Lewis used to say, are final. So, in conclusion, let us,
as it were together with Father John and with Lewis
himself, share in that affirmation of hope which
Lewis, writing from Magdalen College, Oxford, on
14 January 1949, addresses to his "Father most-be-
loved",[26] *Pater dilectissime*, in Verona:

Now indeed mountains and seas divide us; nor
do I know what your appearance is in the
body. God grant, on that day hereafter, day of
the resurrection of the body, yes, and of all
things made, beyond our telling, new—God
grant us, on that Day, to meet.

Afterword

BY LYLE W. DORSETT*

M<small>Y FIRST READING</small> of Martin Moynihan's essay on "The Latin Letters of C. S. Lewis" was as exciting as opening a present from a dear relative who always sent something I treasured and loved. To be sure I knew about these special letters before Mr. Moynihan's effort made the contents public. Indeed, copies of this little collection of epistles are here at the Marion E. Wade Center at Wheaton College, where we have over two thousand of Lewis's

---

*Dr. Lyle W. Dorsett is the curator of the Marion E. Wade Center located at Wheaton College, Wheaton, Illinois. Dr. Dorsett has produced a variety of distinguished works on the history of American culture and politics and is the author of *And God Came In*, a biography of Joy Davidman, wife of C. S. Lewis. The Wade Center is a research center housing an extensive collection of books, manuscripts, letters, and papers of seven well-known British authors: Owen Barfield, G. K. Chesteron, C. S. Lewis, George MacDonald, Dorothy L. Sayers, J. R. R. Tolkien, and Charles Williams.

letters. Nevertheless, I have not used my Latin since I left high school over thirty years ago. Consequently the treasures were hidden until Mr. Moynihan, one of Lewis's pupils at Magdalen College, Oxford, brought them into the light.

With unusual skill, sensitivity, and charm, Martin Moynihan translates and comments on these fascinating letters. An accomplished critic in his own right, Moynihan not only presents excerpts from Lewis's letters to Father Don Giovanni Calabria, but he artfully weaves them together, complete with commentaries that elucidate rather than merely decorate the sources.

Because few theologians, if any, are quoted more from American church pulpits and seminary podiums than C. S. Lewis, almost anything that he wrote attracts attention. But these letters are unusually valuable because they illuminate so many aspects of Professor Lewis's life and work. Among the insights we gain is a glimpse of Lewis's far-flung influence. A somewhat obscure Roman Catholic priest, Don Giovanni Calabria (Father John) read and was touched by *The Screwtape Letters* when the book was translated into Italian in 1947. Like hundreds of other fans of the Oxford author, Father

John wrote to Lewis out of admiration for his work. This began a seven-year correspondence which ended only with the octogenarian priest's death in 1954.

It is unfortunate that C. S. Lewis never kept letters sent to him. Thus only one side of the correspondence survives. This deprivation notwithstanding, we see that Professor Lewis answered his mail punctually and with care, because he believed, as he phrased it in a sermon in 1941, that there are no ordinary people. Young or old, influential or obscure, ignorant or well-educated, Lewis took time to answer each correspondent with thoughtfulness and sensitivity. As a result, Lewis's letters reveal much about him, and they contain some of his most effective teaching.

From Martin Moynihan's essay we learn that while Lewis was not necessarily of one mind with Father John about all of the doctrines of the Roman Catholic Church, he deplored the bigotry of Protestants in Northern Ireland and Catholics in Spain. Furthermore, if Lewis could not embrace all of the Roman Church's teachings, he shared this Italian priest's love for Holy Communion, liturgy, and the church calendar.

Mr. Moynihan demonstrates some other areas of

Christianity that were concerns to C. S. Lewis. The Oxford don joined Father John in seeking unity among all Christians; and it is apparent that Lewis saw schism as a result of sin. From these letters we also find what a high priority Lewis placed on evangelism ("bravely and sweetly bring[ing the] brethren to the Gospel of Christ"); and we see that compassionate service to humankind was equally high on his list of priorities.

The Latin letters remind us of how eclectic Lewis was in his learning and reading. How many people attempt to correspond in a language they do not regularly teach or read, let alone a language like Latin that is considered "dead"? Lewis's wide range of interests in history—both ancient and modern—as well as his familiarity with a broad spectrum of literature—including Scripture, Virgil, Thomas à Kempis and Charles Williams—is equally apparent.

But it is of spiritual matters that we learn even more. Lewis took prayer seriously, and in these pages we have a glimpse of his prayer life. We sense that prayer was not a perfunctory exercise for him. The Latin letters complement what I have learned from several of Lewis's friends: in brief, he excelled in prayer.

One of the most interesting revelations comes from a Christmas letter written in 1951. Here Lewis confides in Father John, revealing that on St. Mark's Day that year he had a strikingly significant experience with God. Lewis confessed that "I long believed that I believed in the forgiveness of sins." But suddenly his heart was warmed and he *knew* it with his "whole heart" for the first time. Was this an experience of second blessing? Was it sanctification? Baptism of the Holy Spirit? Martin Moynihan reminds us that Lewis's expeience was similar to what John Wesley reported happening to himself at Aldersgate Street in London in 1738.

No serious student of C. S. Lewis's life and writings will fail to be enlightened by Martin Moynihan's explication of this little trove of correspondence. I eagerly await publication of his translations of the entire collection. But in the meantime I am grateful for this able scholar's illuminating efforts. I have been edified and instructed. I pray you have too.

Notes

1. Utinam pestifera illa "Renascentia" quam Humanistae efficerent non destruxerit (dum erigere eam se jactabant) Latinum: adhuc possemus toti Europae scribere. (Magdalen College, Oxford. 20 September 1947)
2. Nunc enim curiosi scrutatores omnia nostra effodiunt et veneno publicitatis (ut rem barbaram verbo barbaro nomino) aspergunt. (Magdalene College, Cambridge. 3 January 1961)
3. . . . multum scribis de tuis peccatis. Cave (liceat mihi, dilectissime pater, dicere *cave*) ne humilitas in anxietatem aut tristitiam tanseat. (Magdalen College, Oxford. 26 December 1951)
4. Pontificia Università Lateranense, Focaltà di Sacra Teologia (Tipografia C.B.F., Verona, 1974).
5. The zealous Cahtolic priest and the devout Anglican layman (Corso, p. 83).
6. Ringrazio della fotografia; il suo aspetto è tale e quale mi auguravo: una cosciente gravità armoniosamente composta con una certa vivacità giovanile. Avrò sempre un ricordo nelle mie preghiere per Lui e la vostra Congregazione e spero che anche voi facciate altrettanto per me. (Translated from Latin and quoted by Corso, p. 83. The original has not come to hand.)
7. Pro certo mihi videre vocatus ad missionem specialem in

bonum proximi; . . . Dona mentis et cordis, quibus polles, locum quem tenes coram juvenibus studio addictis, satis perspicua sunt signa divinae erga te voluntatis. Deus a te exspectat ut verbo et opere fratres addeas fortitier et suaviter ad Evangelium Christi. (Casa Buoni Fanciulli, Verona. 18 September 1949)

8. What Lewis himself held regarding the Papacy he does not say. Likely enough he joined with those Anglican divines he admired, and believed in its primacy of honour (though not of jurisdiction). And surely the present Pope's courageous visit to Ireland and his appeal there against terrorism would have confirmed Lewis in that.

   I remember that once we were reading Dryden and we came to that passage in *The Hind and the Panther* (1. 398) where the Panther wishes there were some ultimate authority and then the Hind, looking up to Heaven, says:

   she whom ye seek am I.

   I said I thought that the image of a hind looking up and speaking so was rather incongruous. Lewis disagreed and said he thought it a fine one. Poetry, not theology, was our topic. But I record this as an example of freedom from bias.

9. Disputationes magis aggravant schismata quam sanant: communis operatio, oratio, fortitudo, communes (si Deus voluerit) mortes pro Christo adunabunt. (Magdalen College, Oxford. 25 November 1947)

10. . . . qui enim eadem, ab eisdem, pro erodem, patiuntur, vix possunt non amare inter se. (Magdalen College, Oxford. 20 September 1947)

11. . . . pertransibo cras (si Deo placuerit) in Hiberniam, incunabula mea et dulcissimum refugium quoad amoeni-

tatem locorum et caeli temperiem quamquam nixis et odiis et saepe civilibus armis dissentientium religionum atrocissimam. Ibi sane et vestri et nostri "ignorant quo spiritu ducuntur": carentiam caritatis pro zelo accipiunt et reciprocam ignorantiam pro orthodoxia. (Magdalen College, Oxford. 10 August 1953)

12. . . . verba haec tibi Spiritus dictavit! . . . Te beatum dico et dicam! quod Deus te uti vult ad sua opera explenda. (Casa Buoni Fanciulli, Verona, 3 September 1953)

13. Res mira est corroboratio fidei duas animas loco, natione, lingua, oboedientia, aetate diversas sic in dulcem familiaritatem adductas esse: adeo ordo spirituum ordinem materialem superat. (Magdalen College, Oxford. 17 March 1953)

14. Ipsa naturalis mundi facies jam vere novo renovata proprio modo suo idem jubet (sc. "gaudete!"). (Magdalen College, Oxford. 27 March 1948)

15. Multis aerumnis laboro. Domus mea inquieta, muliebribus rixis vastata, *inter tabernacula Kedar habitandum est.* Grandaeva mater, longa valetudine confecta, diurnae curae mihi est. (Magdalen College, Oxford. 14 January 1949) *muliebribus rixis vastata* (rent with women's quarrels: did Lewis mention this as something Father John was spared? It is interesting that he refers to Mrs Moore as his "aged mother" (*grandaeva mater*). Note the echo of Psalm CXX 5: "Woe is me . . . that I dwell in the tents of Kedar!"

16. Si Deo placuerit ut plura scribam, benedictus sit; si non placuerit, iterum benedictus sit. (*ibidem*)

17. Quoted from my *South of Fort Hertz, A Tale in Rhyme* (Mitre Press, London 1956, p. 11), a verse narrative of the Burma Campaigns (1942-1945).

"The reeking tube" is an 18th-century literary stock-phrase for a gun (as often as not, a fowling piece). In Burma when I first saw our mortars (tubes if ever there were tubes) "begin to speak" and to smoke from rapid fire, I at once called that phrase to mind—and if to mind why not call it back into use, with this double association of past and present?

Lewis himself in his experiences of World War I and of trench warfare in France with the Somerset Light Infantry records how the first time he heard a bullet there came to him "a little quavering signal that said, 'This is War. This is what Homer wrote about.'" (*Surprised by Joy*, Chapter XII, end)

18. Caveamus ne dum frustra de Europae fato cruciamur negligamus aut Veronam aut Oxoniam. In paupere qui ad meam portam pulsat, in matre aegrotante, in iuvene qui consilium meum petit, ipse Dominus adest: ergo ejus pedes lavemus. (Magdalen College, Oxford. 27 March 1948)

19. Diu credebam me credere in remissionem peccatorum. Ac subito (in die S. Marci) haec veritas in mente mea tam manifesto lumine apparuit ut perciperem me numquam antea (etiam post multas confessiones et absolutiones) toto corde hoc credidisse. . . . Fortasse haec liberatio concessa est tuis pro me intercessionibus! (Magdalen College, Oxford. 26 December 1951)

in die S. Marci: 25 April. Compare with Lewis's experience the plaque in Aldersgate Street, London recording the assurance of forgiveness experienced by John Wesley on 24 May 1738.

20. . . . me admodum orphanum esse sentio quia grandaevus meus confessor et carissimus pater in Christo nuper mortem obit. Dum ad altare celebraret subito posto acerrimum sed (Deo gratias) brevissimum dolorem expira-

vit, et novissima verba erant *Venio, Domine Jesu*. (Magdalen College, Oxford. 14 April 1952)

21. The letter on petitionary prayer, written from Magdalen College, Oxford, is dated 14 January 1953. This is one of the letters to which it would be specially interesting to have Father John's reply. Did he perhaps suggest that Our Lord did not bid us pray "nothing doubting" and "Thy will be done" *simultaneously* but *consecutively*? As in the Lord's Prayer, we are to pray the divine Will which *we* do *not* know first, and them make our human petitions. In this, Christ's precept to us differs from His own practice in the Garden of Gethsemane. He *did* know the Will of the Father; and only by praying first for the chalice to pass could He, for our huamnity's sake, pray that at all. As Man and God He prayed this first prayer subordinately; as God and Man He prayed the second superordinately. He knew the Father's Will and He Himself willed it: Calvary. Of course, that the two models are for us to be consecutive (in reverse order) and not simultaneous does not remove the other difficulty which Lewis finds: why, if our prayer is not to be specifically granted, (albeit, in some other, higher way) why, he repeats, are we tantalised, as it were, with assurances of fulfilment that are not to be taken in the letter? Doubtless he thought (ah, woe) of his boyhood petitions for his mother's recovery from illness. The difficulty is made more difficult, he points out, when in some places we are told not that we *shall* receive but that we *have* received. On this, the glosses point to Isaiah: "before ye call I will answer". In the end (and Lewis never doubted the End) we have to be strong in hope, looking for the renewal of all things. Christ's reply to Peter when the Apostles had said "we have left all", is to be pondered.

22. Ora pro me ut Deus mihi concedat aut salutaria aut sal-
    tem haud nocitura dicere. Nam "periculosae plenum
    opus aleae", ut Flaccus scripsit. (Magdalene College,
    Cambridge. 28 March 1959)

23. Fides Christiana, ut puto, magis valet apud Cantabrig-
    gienses quam apud nostros; communistes rariores sunt et
    pestiferi philosophi quos logicales positivistos vocamus
    haud aeque pollent.

    This allusion to Logical Positivism prompts me to
    supplement and modify my contribution to SEVEN,
    Volume V (pp. 101-105), where I said Lewis was per-
    haps wrong in referring to T. D. Weldon as an atheist
    (assuming Weldon it was whom Lewis quotes in *Sur-
    prised by Joy* as saying "it almost looks as if all that stuff of
    Frazer's about the Dying God had really happened
    once"). Recently I have read Sir Alfred Ayer's *A Part of
    my Life;* in it he mentions Weldon and says that he was an
    orthodox Kantian who *later became* "an inflexible linguis-
    tic philosopher". *Surprised by Joy* was published in 1955.
    Thus, writing of the Weldon of the thirties, Lewis may
    have been alluding to an atheism which only developed
    or became explicit after the War.

24. Dr Johnson died on 13 December 1784. He had founded
    The Club—his Inklings, as it were—in 1763. His private
    prayers were published posthumously as "Prayers and
    Meditations" in 1785. In a fine bicentennial article on
    Johnson, "Facing God", published in *The Tablet* of 24
    November 1984, Malcolm Muggeridge quotes John-
    son's last prayer, "which", he adds, "as an octogenarian I
    take on as my own":

    > Almighty and most merciful Father, I am now, as
    > to human eyes it seems, about to commemorate,
    > for the last time, the death of thy son Jesus Christ

our Saviour and Redeemer. Grant, O Lord, that my whole hope and confidence may be in his merits, and his mercy; enforce and accept my imperfect repentance; make this commemoration available to the confirmation of my faith, the establishment of my hope and the enlargement of my charity, and make the death of thy son Jesus Christ effectual to my redemption. Have mercy upon me, and pardon the multitude of my offences. Bless my friends; have mercy upon all men. Support me, by the grace of thy Holy Spirit, in the days of weakness, and at the hour of death, and receive me, at my death, to everlasting happiness, for the sake of Jesus Christ. Amen.

In a Third Leader entitled "An English Saint Remembered", *The Times* recalled that at the approach of death Johnson's final words were Roman and in Latin: (I am now about to die) *jam moriturus*.

Lewis, like Johnson, was versed in the Latin not only of the Fathers but of the Schoolmen. Also, as the Vicar of his church (Holy Trinity, Headington Quarry) told me, he would sometimes come over to the Vicarage and borrow from Canon Head his copy of the renowned scriptural commentaries of the Jesuit commentator, Cornelius de Lapide.

25. Scio vos preces effundere et pro desideratissima uxore mea et pro me qui jam orbatus et quasi dimidiatus solus hanc vallem lacrimorum peragro. (Magdalene College, Cambridge. 8 April 1961)

26. Nunc vero montes et maria nos dividunt nec scio qua sis forma corporis; placeat Deo ut olim in resurrectione corporum et inenarrabili illa novitate congrediamur.

About the Author

MARTIN MOYNIHAN, C.M.G., M.C.

Martin Moynihan was at Magdalen College, Oxford from 1934 to 1938 when C. S. Lewis was Fellow and Tutor in English there. He became Lewis's pupil in English during his fourth year, after reading P.P.E. under T. D. Weldon. He shared in the "beer and Beowulf" evenings and kept in occasional touch after going down. Lewis read the manuscript of Moynihan's verse narrative of the Burma campaigns, *South of Fort Hertz* (published in 1956), characteristically dubbing one passage "a corker". He last saw Lewis after he had attended (with his wife, Monica) Lewis's celebrated Cambridge Inaugural Lecture. Overseas diplomatic service then intervened (Consul-General, Philadelphia; Ambassador, Liberia; High Commissioner, Lesotho) but, on retirement (1976), and with family grown up, he has returned to Lewis—that is, to re-reading him and to reading also the book which Lewis himself read and recommended.

Martin Moynihan is a scholar in his own right, and is presently working on a translation and commentary on the full collection of Lewis's Latin letters for future publication.